Success

Secrets

of a

MILLION $

Party Girl

BY LYNN BARDOWSKI

Jessica Kupferman - Badass Biz
Cover Design
www.badassbiz.com

Clo Brickley
Copy Editor
resumeresc@aol.com

Danielle DiAngelo - AngelEye Photography
Back Cover Photo
www.danielled180angelo.com

Glowing Reviews!

"This book is worth more than a million dollars! You can't put a price on unlocking the secrets to being comfortable in your own skin, and igniting that passion inside of you so you can share your glow with the world! Bardowski's a leading visionista for her time, who makes you want to go out there, live your dreams, while looking good, and enjoying a good glass of wine on the side!"

– The Lady in Red (a.k.a. Laura Madsen)
  TheLadyinRedBlog.com

"Lynn doesn't just tell you how SHE did it—she also tells you how YOU can do it! She really lets you in on her life– the ups AND downs, in an engaging style, while sharing practical tips to help us all become successful. I have been working for 25+ years and still found inspiration to do more and do it better. Read this book!"

– Debbie Moore, Vice President,
  Corporate Communication, Cubist Media Group
  cubistmediagroup.com

"**You will actually get something out of this book.** I've read a lot of self help books for entrepreneurs, and find a lot of them a bit too impractical or heavy laden with ego or nonsense. This is an honest, fun to read blue print toward success which includes resources and a great story of one woman's rise to success. Even though I feel as though I am past a lot of the more simplistic self-helpy women in business books, I did walk away from this one feeling refreshed and inspired. It's a great drink of water if you are having a vision thirsty week! Buy it and send it to friends too!"

– L.L.H., Lynda Hinkle Law lyndahinkle.com

"**I just finished reading the e-book, and feel as if I've captured some of the authors glow.** She has a way of making you feel empowered and able to accomplish whatever you seek. Your attention is captured by her humor, her personal stories, and even her setbacks - you will find answers to questions/conflicts you most certainly have experienced, and most likely will come away with a clearer focus to help you get to where you want to be. Kudos to Lynn Bardowski for an energetic, fun read - thanks for the motivation!"

– Lisa Hargraves

Dedicated to all the women I have met
and have yet to meet along my success journey.

"If you have knowledge, let others light their candles in it."
—Margaret Fuller, journalist, critic,
and women's rights advocate

Visionista, noun

A woman who knows who she is, where she's going,
and guides her tribe of *Leading* Ladies to the top.

Table of Contents

Secret #1
You're Not Who Everyone Thinks You Are

"If you're able to be yourself, then you have no competition.
All you have to do is get closer and closer to that essence."
—Barbara Cook

GROWING UP AT the Jersey Shore, our top tourist attractions were the beach, the bars, and a six-story, ninety-ton elephant. Yes, an elephant. Lucy the Elephant (as she was called) stood just a few blocks from my childhood home in Margate, New Jersey. Lucy was the brainchild of 1881 real estate developer, James V. Lafferty, Jr., who thought that a real estate office inside a giant elephant would attract investors from nearby Atlantic City. A visionary ahead of his time, Lafferty's plan failed, and eventually Lucy was reinvented as a cottage and tavern. By the 1960s, she was an elephant without an identity and fell into disrepair, fated for demolition. Walking past her as a child, I can remember feeling a sense of loss as I watched her tin skin peel away and flap in the wind—the grey paint fading from her gigantic frame. She needed someone to see beyond her deteriorating outside and discover her inner "pachydiva." That rescue came in 1970, when a "Save Lucy" campaign refurbished her to greatness.

I learned my first success secret from Lucy: You're not who everyone thinks you are. It took a hundred years to figure out that Lucy's purpose was not to sell land, but to make people happy. Thank God elephants have thick skin. Today, Lucy is the star of Margate. As a national historic landmark (lucytheelephant.org), she attracts more than 33,000 visitors annually. Lucy doesn't need to be anything other than her true self—a supersized elephant that puts a smile on the faces of locals and tourists alike. One can't help but feel a sense of delight in her unexpected presence among the crashing waves and the smell of the sea, as seagulls fly overhead.

Like Lucy, defining who you are and where you're going is the first step to building your million-dollar business. Hopefully it won't take you a hundred years. We learn many of our ideas about who we are from our childhood, when parents, peers, and teachers let us know exactly who they think we are and what we are capable of. Words like lazy, cute, jock, smart, fat, beautiful, popular, cool, and geek are repeated over and over, until we believe them. We allow the words to define us, giving them permission to chart our life's course. It might have been twenty, thirty, or even forty years ago we heard those labels. Yet, we still hang onto them, forgetting that it's not our story anymore. Those old beliefs hang around our mind, like an old sweater hanging in the back of our closet. It doesn't fit anymore, but we are not quite ready to toss it aside.

The words I heard were beanpole, bookworm, lazy, and quiet. I was a skinny child, a genetic hand-me-down from a distant relative. Cleaning the house or doing dishes was boring to me, so I would conveniently need to use the bathroom when my mom called for help in the kitchen. For some reason, I thought I could hide out there, but of course, she found me. The conversation of adults always interested me; therefore I would quietly listen in and soak up the conversation like my dad's Italian "gravy" in a bowl of spaghetti. Everyone said I was shy and quiet. But I knew I was so much more than what others saw in me. What I didn't know was when or how I would discover the secret to getting the me that was on the inside, out, for the rest of the world to see.

As a child born in the 1960s, the kitchen was the hub that brought our family together for mealtime. Dinner was very Brady Bunch–like (minus Alice, the maid). The menu rotated between pork chops and applesauce, hot dogs and beans, macaroni with Velveeta cheese, pasta fagioli (for my Italian father), and fish sticks. During the school year, our family of six (I have a sister and two brothers) gathered together for breakfast and dinner while my mom instilled her wisdom and molded our young minds. Mom would frequently repeat quotes from two signs that hung on the kitchen wall: "Be who you is because if you be who you ain't, than you ain't who you is" and "Be sure brain is in gear before engaging mouth." I can see her standing in the kitchen and hear her voice as I write this. When adolescence loomed, Judy Blume books such as, *Are You There God? It's Me, Margaret*, started appearing in our home, which were my mom's backup for all the answers to growing up and feeling inadequate.

It all sounded great until I approached my teenage years, when my eye-rolling began. The reality was that the pretty girls with boobs got everything a teenage girl could wish for, including dates to the school dance and invitations to all the popular parties. I knew this because my younger sister (by fourteen months), Lori, inherited the good looks and boobs genes. She got picked for cheerleading, had the attention of all the cute boys, and was one of the popular girls. If only I had great hair and boobs, my life would be perfect. Flat-chested girls didn't have much fun. I wasted a lot of time wanting to be prettier, more popular, and waiting for my boobs to develop. I even did those silly arm exercises that were meant to increase the size of your bust. There was a mantra to go along with the exercise, "We must, we must, we must increase our bust." I repeated the mantra with enthusiasm and vigor, waiting for nature to kick in. I'm still waiting.

On my first day of high school, I showed up looking like a dork with glasses and braces, which motivated me to want to make money for a new wardrobe. It was time to get a job and reinvent my look. Prudential Insurance, which was conveniently located across the street from the high school, was the answer. My mom worked there and had an "in" that landed me a job on a special project, working twenty hours a week before school. With a steady income coming in, I was suddenly flush with cash. For the first time in my life I could buy almost any clothes I wanted. I stocked up on hip-huggers and bell-bottoms, which were all the rage. Fashion became my passion. Dreams of opening my own store (with windows that resembled a Vogue fashion shoot) filled my mind, as I gazed into the junior clothing stores at the mall.

My three siblings and I lived right outside the two-mile requirement to ride the bus, so we had to walk, ride a bike, or find a ride. Retelling the stories of how I walked to school in the dead of winter has come in handy for teaching my children lessons on how easy their life is. Some days back then I'd get lucky and hitch a ride from my dad in his TastyKake (a snack cake company) truck. That's when I discovered how to get the me that was on the inside, out to the rest of the world. I suddenly noticed other people's reaction to my dad. Respected people in our community walked up to my dad with a big smile and treated him like he was very important. They'd share a story with me of how they met him and what a great man he was. Suddenly my dad looked taller and more impressive to me. He had a "presence." The answer was in front of me the whole time. I felt like Dorothy discovering I could have clicked my ruby red slippers together to get home anytime I wanted. I defined who I was (although, a cool wardrobe did go a long way with the high school crowd). My dad didn't let what people saw on the outside, a deliveryman in a truck and uniform, define who he was on the inside. He decided who he was, the CEO of his own cake route. People reacted to his persona, a man with integrity and character who looked you in the eyes and shook your hand with respect. My dad served people, not snack cakes.

Mr. Tasty, as my dad was called, knew everyone in town by their first name. Even though he retired more than twenty years ago, my dad is still recognized every time we go somewhere. People remember him because he always made them feel valued. In addition to providing me with unlimited Krimpets (their top-selling snack cake), my dad taught me that how I saw myself is how others would see me. He encouraged me to let everyone else see the strong, smart, confident girl that he saw. I put my toe in the water, and little by little I stopped thinking about the things I couldn't change (like my hair) and focused on things I could change, like people's perception of me, and the unique gifts I brought to the world. That which comes from within is our true power.

Fashion continued to interest me throughout high school. I was encouraged to attend a small junior college in the Delaware

Valley. After two years, I received my associate degree and transferred to the University of Delaware to work toward my bachelor of science degree. During that time I started to date a childhood friend of the family, Bill. After our first date, I woke my mother up to tell her that Bill was the man I was going to marry. One month before I was set to leave for UD, my relationship with Bill became more serious, and I didn't want to go away to school. After all, Bill was the man of my dreams. I told my very disappointed mother that if I could get a job in my field with my associate degree, I was not going back to school. There was no stopping a crazy-in-love, know-it-all, twenty-year-old girl.

I quickly applied to the fashion retail stores in the area and got a job managing Ormond's, a women's clothing chain store at the Shore Mall. By Christmas, Bill and I were engaged, and we married the following fall. My name badge announced my new title and formalized my married name, Mrs. Bardowski, Assistant Store Manager. Like my hair in the 1980s, my dreams were BIG. I pictured myself owning a boutique in the city, or as a buyer for a big department store, looking stylish and successful.

It didn't take long for my retail honeymoon to end. I came home many nights from work frustrated and unfulfilled, crying to my new husband about apathetic part-timers, shoplifters, low pay, and long hours. One dark, cold night I walked out into an empty parking lot to find that my car had been stolen. The last straw came when I got caught in a rainstorm and my moussed, teased, sprayed-out big hair became a flat, tangled mess. As I ran past the store windows, I could see my reflection in the glass. The unrecognizable twenty-something, mess-of-a-woman was me. Looking at my reflection, I knew that my life's purpose was supposed to be more than this. I just didn't know how to find it.

My big brother, Mike, came to the rescue by offering advice. Like me, he got a job in retail after college, managing Radio Shack at the mall. We'd meet up frequently at Capri Pizza (the mall hang out) to share our retail war stories. Mike lasted through the Christmas season, and then he packed up and moved to Maryland to follow his dreams and his girlfriend. Loyalty must run in the family. Mike was having success and earning big commissions as a printing sales rep. Even though it was a male-dominated field (there were no women sales reps in his office) he encouraged me to give it a try. I was so miserable, I figured I had nothing to lose, so I scoured the help-wanted ads, never considering if I'd even like a sales rep job. No one wanted to hire a corporate sales rep with no corporate sales experience; therefore I took the only outside sales job I could find, which was selling custom mirrors to homeowners. If you want something bad enough, be willing to let go of your ego long enough to take any job that will be a launching pad to living your dream. Everyone has to start somewhere.

After one year of sales experience, I got hired as a printing sales rep for a small Philadelphia company. I soon learned that I was not like everyone else. Printing sales was an industry dominated by men, all of them wearing the same navy blue suit, white shirt, and tie. While waiting to meet with my client, I frequently received condescending glances from the male sales reps. At first I thought being a woman, especially a young inexperienced woman, was a weakness. Would anyone take me seriously? It turns out that my "ness" was my secret weapon. According to morewords.com (a useful guide for playing *Words With Friends*) there are 2,874 words that end with "ness." Some of my favorites are adroitness, differentness, uniqueness, smartness, awesomeness, wondrousness (I really like that one) and bitchiness, which my friend re-invented as "babe in total control of herself."

Find the words that define you and how you want to be perceived. Put them on a vision board, photo board, or on your refrigerator so that you can see them every day. When the doubter creeps in, use the words as reminders of who you really are.

Instead of hiding myself in navy blue suits so I'd look the part like the rest of the sales reps, I embraced my individuality and wore clothes that were true to my authentic self. After all, I still loved fashion. One of my favorite outfits was a hot pink skirt and jacket. The navy suits couldn't miss me. Dressing as my true self in clothes that I loved, not only empowered me; it drew people to me because it changed my attitude. I wasn't hiding anymore. Break free from the crowd and embrace what makes you unique. Do people see who you really are, or are you still hiding behind a limiting belief that might have never been true in the first place? My wardrobe showed that I was not afraid to take a risk. I closed the big accounts using my creativity, sharing innovative ideas, and exceeding expectations. When one of my Customers called to say that they were about to run out of custom envelopes, I sprang into action, rushed the order, and personally delivered it by day's end.

By the time I was twenty-seven, we were approaching a new decade. I worked hard to have it all—a wonderful husband, two daughters, live-in nanny, successful sales career, and the big house that went with it. Everything looked great on the outside, but something was still missing. I began to question if this was what success was all about. Deciding where to put corporate logos on payroll checks was a long way from the fashion world

I had dreamed about as a teen, even if I could wear pink suits. I had turned into a guilt-ridden, working mom full of frustration, leaving my children every morning to go work for someone else and sell a product that I wasn't even excited about. The income was great, but money doesn't buy fulfillment. Turns out it bought me a live-in nanny to do what I wanted to be doing myself, baking cookies with my daughters and playing on the swings in the park. I went in search of a home-based business that would fuel my passion while giving me the flexibility to be a mom.

This is my story of how I discovered my inner Visionista —overcoming fear, failure, and mommy guilt to build a multi-million-dollar business. The principles are universal and can be applied to any business venture, or adventure. Come along with me and enjoy the journey.

LYNN BARDOWSKI

NOTES:

WHO ARE YOU?

LYNN BARDOWSKI

NOTES:

WHO ARE YOU?

Secret #2
Wealthy People Turn Pages

"Great minds discuss ideas; average minds discuss events;
small minds discuss people."
—Eleanor Roosevelt

WHILE IMPARTING HER favorite quotes, my mom also taught us to expand our minds by taking us to the library, which was just a few blocks away. She impressed upon us that reading was the key to knowledge. When I turned thirteen, she gave me a treasured classic, *Little Women*, which I still have today. On the inside page she wrote, "Happy Birthday Teenager. Thank you, for being you!" Louisa May Alcott's story about the March sisters peaked my interest in reading and left me wanting more. I started to pick up books and magazines that were gathering dust on the coffee table in the living room, including *Reader's Digest*. The powder blue velvet swivel chair positioned next to the bay window was my favorite reading spot during the summer. I'd curl up and swivel back and forth as the sun poured through the window, escaping into a world of adventure, drama, and humor.

The *Reader's Digest* "Word Power" expanded my vocabulary. I embraced learning and exercised my mind, as I practiced my new word for the week. Too bad we didn't have the *Words With Friends* game back then; I could have easily scored the fifty+ pointers.

The *Reader's Digest* "All in a Day's Work" taught me to see the humor in everyday situations. I learned that life is too short to take work, or ourselves, too seriously. The stories, which were sent in by real people, were hysterical. Many times I'd catch myself laughing out loud, before we had LOL to express ourselves. Maybe that's where I got the idea that work should be a party.

The *Reader's Digest* "Drama in Real Life" stories about survival, determination, perseverance, and hope kept me on the edge of my chair, and many times brought tears to my eyes. My biggest teenage drama was not fitting in with the cool crowd or not having a date to the dance. That wasn't such a big deal after I read about someone surviving a plane crash or terminal illness. The memories of those stories still keep me grounded when I start to stress over the little things. Somewhere out there, someone is fighting for their life. My stuff stressful? Not so much.

One day, I read an article in *Reader's Digest* that inspired me to be an Entrepreneur. The article was about real estate investing. Back in 1975, you could buy an average home for about $35,000. The author explained that you could rent the home out to pay for the mortgage and sell it ten years later for a big profit. If I started now at age thirteen, I'd be rich by the time I was twenty-three! Ten years seemed like light-years away, but I thought I could at least make enough to start saving for a car. I asked my dad for a loan, expecting an enthusiastic "Yes!" If *Reader's Digest* thought it was a great idea, I knew my dad would agree. Sadly, I got my first big "No," and I also learned that teenagers couldn't qualify for a bank loan. *Reader's Digest* was just the appetizer. I was ready to move on to the main course and learn more about motivation and Entrepreneurship, adding *Think and Grow Rich* and *How to Win Friends and Influence People* to my reading library. Both books were published in the 1930s. Although I read them more than forty years later, those books still stand the test of time today and are frequently recycled by many motivational speakers and authors, including me.

Think and Grow Rich (the original *Secret*), by Napoleon Hill, was a "how to create abundance" book based on Hill's studies of wealthy people, including Andrew Carnegie. Carnegie believed that your thoughts, expectations, and desire determined your opportunity and fortune. Simply put, what you focus on is what you get. Carnegie said, "The man who acquires the ability to take full possession of his own mind may take possession of anything else to which he is justly entitled." Reading that my thoughts could control my destiny was pretty cool stuff to think about for a teenager. It became part of my belief system and changed my future.

Another famous Carnegie, Dale, wrote *How to Win Friends and Influence People*. While doing research for this book, I found out that he changed his name from Carnagey to Carnegie for name recognition (*dalecarnegie.org) Maybe that's how he won friends and influenced people. One of his tips is to win people over to your way of thinking by letting them think that they thought of the idea. Women are masters of this technique. I watched my mom do this for years with my dad. Another tip is to see the situation from the other person's point of view. Or, as my mother would say, "You never know someone until you walk a mile in their shoes." She could have written that book, although changing her name from Cusack to Carnegie would have been a stretch.

During my high school years, I expanded my collection of books to include my new interest in fashion. I added *W* magazine and *Minding the Store*, by Stanley Marcus. Published in 1974, *Minding the Store* should be required reading for every Entrepreneur. Stanley Marcus seemed larger than life to me. The book left a lasting impression, teaching me many business gems, including: "There is never a good sale for Neiman Marcus unless it's a good buy for the Customer;" or "...quality is remembered long after the price is forgotten;" and "... if a product doesn't fit in your store, or isn't at the appropriate taste level for your brand, the more you sell of it, the worse it is." The last lesson about branding is even more relevant in this economy.

Want to know how to brand your biz? Read *Minding the Store*. Stanley Marcus was a genius.

Reading *Minding the Store* changed the direction of my life, as books will do. It's what sparked my interest to get a degree in Fashion Merchandising. When my daughter, Alyssa, was sixteen she had a similar experience when she read *The Devil Wears Prada*. The book ignited her dream to work in New York City and charted her future. Today, she's a city girl, working in Midtown Manhattan, right across the street from Cartier.

Books kept me inspired during my transition into corporate sales. I gained insight on determination, leadership, communication, and courage from reading *On Wings of Eagles*, by Ken Follett; *Lincoln*, by Gore Vidal; *Iacocca*, by Lee Iacocca with William Novak; and *Alive: The Story of the Andes Survivors*, by Piers Paul Read.

When I became an Entrepreneur, I continued to build my library.

HERE ARE MY READING SUGGESTIONS:

All You Can Do, Is All You Can Do, But All You Can Do Is Enough! – A.L. Williams

Delivering Happiness: A Path to Profits, Passion, and Purpose – Tony Hsieh

Developing the Leader Within You – John C. Maxwell

Developing the Leaders Around You: How to Help Others Reach Their Full Potential – John C. Maxwell

Endless Referrals – Bob Burg

Even Eagles Need A Push – David McNally

Fish! – Stephen C. Lundin, PhD, John Christensen, Harry Paul, and Ken Blanchard

Go For No! – Richard Fenton and Andrea Waltz

Little Red Book of Selling – Jeffrey H. Gitomer

Mojo – Marshall Goldsmith

Peaks and Valleys – Spencer Johnson, MD

Steve Jobs – Walter Isaacson

Take Big Bites – Linda Ellerbee

The Aladdin Factor – Jack Canfield and Mark Victor Hansen

The Color Code – Taylor Hartman, PhD

The Heart of a Leader – Ken Blanchard

The Millionaire Mind – Thomas J Stanley, PhD

The Power of Focus – Jack Canfield, Mark Victor Hansen, and Les Hewitt

The Secret, What Great Leaders Know and Do – Ken Blanchard, Mark Miller

The Secret – Rhonda Byrne

The Success Principles – Jack Canfield and Janet Switzer

Touch the Top of the World – Erik Weihenmayer

Unstoppable – Cynthia Kersey

Where Have All the Leaders Gone? – Lee Iacocca

Who Moved My Cheese? – Spencer Johnson, MD

The E Myth: Why Most Businesses Don't Work and What to Do About It – Michael E. Gerber

Social Media makes it even easier to learn, as friends and colleagues share and post content on Facebook, Linkedin, and Twitter. The Zite app is my morning reading source on my iPhone and iPad. I can customize topics and have content served up with my morning coffee, all based on my interests. Zite also makes it easy to share content. So when I read something that is shareworthy, I can tap and tweet in the blink of an eye. That in turn, builds my Twitter followers.

If you really want to absorb what you learn and grow exponentially, teach what you learn to someone else. Many of the books I mentioned above have turned into discussion topics for my training classes, workshops, webcasts, and teleconferences. This book is the sum of all my experience and knowledge.

Nature is smarter than we are. While we're looking for the miracle-grow fertilizer, many of the most beautiful plants and trees take years to develop and bloom. They need to absorb just the right amount of sunlight and water to flourish. Turns out, people do, too—thriving and expanding as their minds absorb new ideas. Information leads to creative thought, inspired action, and vision.

NOTES:

Secret #3
Act On Purpose

"I've always taken risks, and never worried what the world
might really think of me."
—Cher

I SPENT THE 1980S chasing the mighty dollar. The more I
chased, the more my purpose ran away from me. Every job I
took was a climb up the baby boomer ladder to success. After
all, wasn't that what we were all here for, to reach the top rung?
I jumped from retail to corporate sales like an automated robot
with a predetermined program, never considering what I really
wanted out of life or what my purpose was. I thought life was
all about having more "stuff"—a big house, fancy car, expensive
wardrobe, and a live-in nanny to care for my two daughters,
Lauren and Alyssa.

By 1989, Bill and I were living in a four-bedroom home
with a two-car garage, mauve carpets (the hot color trend in carpets), a study, and a family room with a deck outside the sliding
doors. Everyone in the "burbs" was getting a deck, so of course;
we had to have one, too. Madonna was singing about virgins
while my girlfriends and I all wanted what Meg Ryan was having in a New York deli (*When Harry Met Sally*). The daughters of

19

liberated, bra-burning women of the 1960s embraced newfound careers and opportunities. My generation bought into the "You Can Have IT All" motto, meaning a career, kids, home, husband, and a dog. We forgot to add sleep to the list. I woke up one day and wanted to give "IT All" back; mommy guilt was seeping in. Where was the return department for full-time careers? What I really wanted was to be home with my daughters. There had to be a home-based business out there where I could use my creativity, and somehow make a difference in the world. Like many women, I kept quiet about my mommy guilt for two reasons: (1) I worked hard to get where I was and (2) we needed my income to afford our lifestyle. With a mortgage to pay and a company car to replace, starting a business was a big risk. The recession of the early 1990s was looming, the real estate market was taking a dive, and there were rumors about a possible war in the Gulf. How could I even begin to let my husband know how unhappy I was, when the timing to start a business could not have been worse?

Then it happened, at a moment when I was least expecting it. My purpose and passion were revealed, as if a magician took a black cape and swirled it around and announced, Voilà! The magic came in the form of an invite to "one of those" home parties. I was more of a demo snob than a demo diva, but the invite was from my sister-in-law, Denise, who had just started a candle and home decor direct-selling business. I surreptitiously envied her because she was able to be home with her children who were the exact age as my three- and five-year-old daughters. Today that's called a "mom-preneur." Back then, we just said "work-at-home mom," which I think is really an oxymoron. Every mom who is home is working her butt off.

My husband gave me a new invention as an early Christmas gift that year, something called a cellular phone. It was the size of our home phone and was installed permanently into the console. Back then, talking on your car phone was a status symbol, not a violation of the law. Denise would call to chat about our daughters or make plans to meet up over the weekend, so they could play. Denise was home baking Christmas cookies with her children while I was out on the road meeting with clients and closing deals. Baking sounded like a much better idea. I allowed myself to daydream for a moment and pictured myself in the kitchen, combining flour and sugar as Lauren and Alyssa cracked the eggs and mixed the batter. Since I was never known for my cooking or baking skills, it must have been my mommy guilt germinating. Like the *Invasion of the Body Snatchers*, it was beginning to take over.

Forced to attend the party out of family obligation, and secretly intrigued to find out more, I ventured out into the unknown. It was my first candle party. The minute I walked in the door, I was hooked. What was that wonderful fragrance? They had me at raspberry! I felt like I was Monty Python, discovering the Holy Grail after a long quest. Deep down in my gut, I knew this was what I had been looking for. The women around me at the party were having fun, thankful to have an opportunity to connect with each other and take a break from their busy lives. There were happy, joyful faces making true connections. I wanted what they were having, and I didn't have to fake it like Meg Ryan.

As I smelled the fragrances, I realized candles were present everywhere in my life. It was like when you buy a new car and you suddenly see the same car in the same color everywhere on the road. Whether I was entertaining friends and family, enjoying romantic dinners with my husband, praying, or celebrating a special occasion, I always lit a candle. When I had a stressful day, I lit a candle to unwind and relax. Funny, I had never thought about it before.

Sometimes your life's purpose can be right in front of you. Be open to the fact that it might be disguised as something else. Fashion always meant clothing to me, but now my eyes opened up to the possibilities of using my creativity and passion to build a home fashion business. Candles were much more than a product to sell. They made the room, and more importantly, the women, glow. It was as if I was seeing one of my favorite quotes come to life, "A candle loses none of its light by lighting another candle"— Unknown. My purpose was right there in front of me, waiting for me to open my eyes and see the light.

I would have never dreamed in a million years that I'd grow up to be a "demonstrator," as they were called in 1990. That's not a label I wanted for myself, and I certainly didn't want other people seeing me that way. After all, my ego said, "You're a successful corporate sales rep with a BMW as a company car. Don't give up the status." Then I thought of my dad in his TastyKake uniform, walking tall as the successful "CEO of life" he chose to be. My dad taught me to find my passion, even if it wasn't what other people thought I should be doing, and give it my best. One of his famous dad quotes was, "I don't care if your dream is to be a garbage man, be the best garbage man there is." (I knew he really meant garbage woman.)

I had to get out of my own way, leave my ego at the door, and follow my heart, which was racing with possibilities. However, this would mean that I'd have to go from riches to rags and give up many of the comforts my income afforded my family and me. There would be no more boutique shopping or designer duds for Lauren and Alyssa, at least not for a while. I walked away from the party, inspired to share my glow and empower other women to discover theirs. My inner Visionista was just beginning to wake up. Together, we'd make dreams come true. I couldn't wait to get home and tell Bill that I was going to start my own business and quit my corporate sales job. As I looked through the windshield at the road ahead, I knew my future was about to change. My doubter tried to creep in with her "what if" scenarios, but I kept her at bay, letting my inner Visionista guide me home. I was ready to act - on purpose.

NOTES:

MY PURPOSE IS...

Secret #4
Pack Your Golden Lasso

"The most effective way to do it, is to do it."
—Amelia Earhart

SOMETHING MAGICAL HAPPENS when you discover your purpose. You might look like an ordinary, mild-mannered mom, wife, or coworker, but you're not. You've changed. You've found a bigger purpose that's guiding your life. It can be very hard to explain to friends and family members, who will most likely think you're crazy. Bill was one of them. I bounced through the door and announced with great enthusiasm that I was going to quit my job to start a business selling candles in people's homes. Yay me! Or, as we said in the 1990s, Awesome! Bill's entire face fell to the floor, like a cartoon character that had been hit on the head with an anvil. I was feeling like Wonder Woman and my husband just became The Villain. Where was my golden lasso when I needed it?

The alter ego of the super hero is always an ordinary person, just like you and me. All they need is a phone booth, bat cave, or golden lasso to harness extraordinary powers and transform them. We all have super hero powers waiting to be revealed, along with villains who try to destroy them. The villain could be disguised as a close friend, family member, or even ourself, but the villain is almost always motivated by one thing: FEAR. That's why people you don't know will be more supportive of your new business than people you know. Acquaintances have nothing to fear whether you fail or succeed. They'll be your biggest cheerleaders. When I told my hairdresser about my new business, she could not have been happier for me, and even volunteered to host a party. My mother, on the other hand, thought it was a horrible idea and feared for my future, suggesting I should get a job as a teacher if I wanted to spend more time with children. Teaching was a safe, secure, and respected profession, with a pension. What crazy person would give up a high-paying job with a company car? Apparently, me.

Bill's response had nothing to do with his lack of support or love for me. It was the villain, fear, trying to destroy my newfound Entrepreneur super powers. I realized his fear was fueled by his own belief system. We lived at the level of our incomes, so he expressed his fear of being able to pay our bills. We could lose everything we worked so hard to gain, and even worse, face financial ruin. My first thought was, "Who invited Debbie Downer (*Saturday Night Live*) to my big reveal?" When he put it that way, I started to let fear creep in, too. He took the wind right out of my sails, as many people will do along your success journey, including those who are closest to you.

Bill and I decided on a compromise. I would not quit my job until I developed a sales team and was earning a consistent income. This approach sounded fair, considering that my weekly paycheck was needed to pay the bills. We cut back on expenses to prepare for our new budget, canceling everything from the Disney channel to the daily newspaper. My lifestyle changed drastically, from shopping at boutiques to searching for bargains at Walmart. At the end of the day, it was all just "stuff."

Don't put your dream on hold while you wait to get support from family members and friends. The support you are craving is probably not going to happen. If you want to destroy the villain, believe in yourself and your powers. Let your purpose and passion be your guide, and act on it. Your hero is living inside of you, just waiting for you to find your golden lasso, cape, mojo, "ness" , whatever you want to call it. It's that moment when we go from ordinary to extraordinary. We look the same, but we know that deep inside something has changed. There's an energy that radiates from deep within our soul, lighting up the room like fireworks on the 4th of July—or, in my case, candlelight. You'll get your husband's support when you can show him a big paycheck.

Surround yourself with people who believe in you, even when the doubter creeps in. Wonder Woman had Wonder Girl; Superman had Lois; and Batman had Alfred, the butler. I turned to two women who I knew were already building successful businesses for their mentoring and guidance, Gail and Denise. They believed in me.

Feel the fear and do it anyway became my daily affirmation. According to Neal Donald Walsch, fear means "false evidence appearing real." It really is all in our head. So, what is your head telling you? Fear of success and fear of failure are the two biggest factors that stop us from moving forward, based on those old limiting beliefs. We're not good enough, we don't deserve it, and we don't have enough certifications or degrees next to our name, blah, blah, blah. To make sure we don't have to face our fear, we typically sabotage ourselves and wonder why we never get where we're going, playing the blame game. It must be the economy, the weather, lack of support, or somebody's fault other than our own. The one thing that's holding you back is probably looking at you in the mirror. Grizzly bears are something to fear, hypothetical situations, and "what if's" are all made up in that space between our ears. Think of the time we waste pondering all the worst case, "what if" scenarios, becoming a human version of Chicken Little running around waiting for the sky to fall. Don't be afraid. The sky is not falling.

Motivated by my heart's desire to not miss another day in my daughters' lives, and my eagerness to put my passion into action, I got to work. There was no time to go for a test run and have an "if it works, I'll quit my day job" attitude. I had to go all in and commit. After all, if I didn't believe in myself enough to go all in, why should anyone else? I had to take a leap of faith, jump off the edge, and figure out how to build my wings on the way down.

I had no idea how I was going to do it, but I had the why. When you have a big why, you'll figure out the how. Don't get caught up feeling that you need to know everything to start your business. "Enthusiasm on fire is better than knowledge on ice." – Author unknown. I didn't know what I didn't know. But neither did anyone else. My passion became contagious, and within six weeks I was developing new Entrepreneurs and Leading a Team. My mentors guided me along the way, "showing" instead of "telling" me how to lead others.

Instead of devoting my time to learning product names, and pricing, I decided to focus on the bigger picture—people development. Keep in mind that this was before Google, Facebook, and e-mail (somewhere between dinosaurs and plasma TVs).

Being a bookworm for all those years served my team and me well. Somewhere in my brain, all the lessons I learned from reading *Think and Grow Rich*, *Minding the Store*, *How to Win Friends and Influence People*, *Reader's Digest*, and even *Little Women* were right in front of me. It was as if I was Tom Hanks in the *Da Vinci Code*, at the moment when he visualizes the orbs in front of him and realizes it was Newton's apple that was the missing orb (Cue music). I unknowingly spent years studying for this moment, and the answers were all there for me to see. The switch that turned on the light was my purpose and passion.

Armed with my golden lasso, my belief, my mentors, and a team of excited new Entrepreneurs to lead, my big dream was clearly in sight.

Even so, continuing to work my corporate job and devote time to building a new business was beginning to take a toll on our family. I worked Monday through Friday selling printing, and focused on my business on the weekends. It seemed counterintuitive, considering my end goal was to spend more time with my children. Mommy guilt was definitely back. By summer, something had to give. I was ready to say goodbye to printing sales forever. Living near the beach motivated me even more. I gave my two-week notice, handed in the keys to my BMW, and told Lauren and Alyssa we would be spending our summer with the sand between our toes, visiting our old friend, Lucy the Elephant. My first day off the job, we packed up the car with buckets and shovels and headed east to celebrate our newfound freedom. As I held two small hands and gazed out over the expansive ocean, my thoughts were drawn to the horizon and the unlimited possibilities that lay ahead.

NOTES:

MY WHY IS…

Secret #5
Inside Every Woman Lives a Million $ Party Girl

"Whatever you choose, however many roads you travel, I hope
that you choose not to be a lady. I hope you will find some way
to break the rules and make a little trouble out there. And I
also hope that you will choose to make some of that trouble on
behalf of women."
—Nora Ephron

SPEAKING WITH THOUSANDS of Entrepreneurs
and Leaders over the last twenty-two years has revealed a
common thread; most women don't know the difference between
a vision and a goal. According to an article entitled "Women
and the Vision Thing" in the *Harvard Business Review,* "Women
scored lower on envisioning—the ability to recognize new
opportunities and trends in the environment and develop a new
strategic direction for an enterprise."

Like many of my friends, I was taught at a young age that
nice girls don't toot their own horn. We were supposed to act
like a lady. My mom's generation sacrificed for family, God, and
country while men took charge of business. How many women

Entrepreneurs with vision did you learn about in history class? Right off the top of my head, I can't think of any. John D. Rockefeller, Thomas Edison, and Andrew Carnegie are the first that come to mind when I think of Entrepreneurs with vision. I would have loved to have heard the story of Coco Chanel (born in 1883) as I was sitting in sixth-grade social studies; however, businessmen dominated the pages of my history book. My role models were women who changed history such as Helen Keller, Susan B. Anthony, and Harriet Tubman. We need more Visionistas in the history books. Even when I was researching success quotes for this book I found that the majority of quotes in the "Googleverse" are from men. To find quotes from women, I had to search by their specific name. It's our time to step out, take center stage, and make some noise.

One day, while enjoying my newfound mommy-ness, inspiration appeared at the drive-through window, as I picked up Happy Meals for Lauren and Alyssa. The sign over the big yellow arch appeared in front of me like a flashing billboard: BILLIONS and BILLIONS SERVED.

When you're open to receiving inspired thoughts, they can come from a very unlikely source, even from a fast-food restaurant. That was it! I had to put my vision on a "sign" and share it with others! No matter what you think about McDonald's food, Ray Kroc was an innovative genius. There had to be something I could glean from his example. As soon as the kids got through lunch, we were off to the library (Google wasn't born yet) so that I could learn as much as possible about Ray Kroc's story. (It turns out that hamburgers and candles have a lot in common.)

There are five lessons Ray Kroc taught me that inspired me to rock my inner Visionista:

1. **You don't need to invent a new or innovative product.** What you do need is passion! Candles and hamburgers are not new products. Burgers have been around since the late 1800s, and candles date back to the Egyptians. Ray Kroc didn't even invent McDonald's. He was selling milk shake machines when he walked into the McDonald's brothers' restaurant and had his "Aha!" moment. Inspired by Henry Ford's assembly line process, Ray Kroc was passionate about the systems the McDonald brothers created, and the potential for sharing the business concept with others. "When I saw it working that day in 1954, I felt like some latter-day Newton who'd just had an Idaho potato caromed off his skull," Ray Kroc said. "That night in my motel room I did a lot of heavy thinking about what I'd seen during the day. Visions of McDonald's restaurants dotting crossroads all over the country paraded through my brain." (That was exactly how I felt when I walked into that party smelling those raspberry candles.)

2. **It's never too late to get started.** Ray Kroc was fifty-two years old when he opened his first McDonald's franchise. He bought the rights to the business a few years later. Thanks to Ray Kroc, I knew I had plenty of time to leave my mark on the world. Even now, after turning fifty this year, I feel like I am just getting started. Isn't fifty the new thirty?

3. **We succeed by empowering others to succeed.** Ray Kroc believed that it was up to him to support every

business owner, and he poured his energy into developing people. He succeeded by giving his franchisees the tools and training they needed to succeed, as if he worked for them. Imagine if corporate managers embraced this concept with their employees? It would revolutionize most businesses. In other words, "A candle loses none of its light by lighting another candle." He was speaking to me.

4. **Create your vision and put it on a sign for the world to see.** The McDonald's sign was Ray Kroc at his best. It takes a lot of chutzpah to put your vision out there in such a big way that everyone knows who you are and, more importantly, where you're going. There was always an expectation that the number on the McDonald's sign would go up. We'd drive by as kids and look with eager anticipation to see how many more burgers were served. The entire nation was rooting for McDonald's to be a success. Today the sign simply says, Billions and Billions Served.

5. **Visionaries change the world.** Inspired by Ray Kroc's philanthropy, the local Philadelphia franchises donated the proceeds of the Shamrock Shake to build the first Ronald McDonald House in 1974. Today there are more than 300 Ronald McDonald Houses all over the world, providing comfort, care, and support to families. The abundance we create is like throwing a rock in a pond. The ripple starts small but gains size and momentum as it grows past the center. The lives you touch can impact thousands, if not millions of people.

I didn't get the Million $ Party Girl Starter Kit, I got the same one everyone else did. It's not what you have; it's what you do with it. After nine months in business, I was ready to give birth to a new vision. But I was at a loss when people asked me, "What do you do?" Today, that's called your elevator pitch. In 1990, a pitch was something girls did playing softball. Therefore, as a women Entrepreneur, I had no idea of where to start. How could I introduce myself so that people took me seriously and really "got" where I was going? Many of my mentors called themselves a Candle Lady or a Demonstrator (yuck). That was so 1970s. Hadn't we come a long way, baby? As a business owner, I recruited, coached, and trained a sales team, developed Leaders, planned events, created a marketing strategy, and gave motivational speeches, all while selling candles and home decor at home parties. I was going for something bigger. Entrepreneur? Mom-Preneur? Work-at-home mom? What was I?

All I knew was that my vision was to share my glow, and empower hundreds of women to discover theirs. I decided on the title of "Nationwide Developer." Hey, I was the CEO, so why not give myself a title deserving of my skills? After all, my energy was focused on looking for talented, motivated, candle-loving Entrepreneurs to join my growing (and glowing) team. We had no territories—the nation was our oyster. My new title drew people in and encouraged them to find out more about me. Now I just had to figure out how to communicate my vision to the masses.

If Ray Kroc could start a new biz at the age of fifty-two, my expectations were even bigger at age thirty. I was ready to break some rules! At that time, no one in my area had built a million-dollar business within his or her first few years, but that didn't mean it couldn't be done. Someone had to be the first. I needed a visual, my version of the golden arches. I grabbed a magic marker and poster board and drew what a million-dollar business would look like in my world. My poster had eight circles on it to represent each future new Leader (we didn't have any—yet) who would be joining me on the journey to creating a million-dollar business. It called out like a "Leaders with Vision" wanted sign. I invited everyone over to announce my new vision and share how it would impact our team—each woman's success would lead the way for others to follow. We were going to be trailblazers; create a new region, and generate one million in annual revenue! Woo-hoo! Two unexpected things happened: (1) my vision inspired people to act and (2) people wanted to follow a Leader who was going to take them somewhere. One by one, the women came up to take the black marker and write their name in one of the circles. They claimed their right to dream big! It was an empowering and powerful moment.

Each future Leader received their own poster to create their vision on. They drew out what it would take to move up and build their teams, using circles to represent their dream team. The momentum had begun! We were propelled by forward motion, and there was no stopping us. Who is on your dream team that will propel your vision forward? Who do you still need to find?

I shared my vision at every opportunity. When someone asked me, "What do you do?" I passionately announced that I was a Talent Scout, building a million-dollar sales team in New Jersey. If I was in Philly, I said I was developing Pennsylvania. If I was in Maryland, I was developing Maryland. I was the same person whether I introduced myself as a Candle Lady or a Talent Scout, developing an entire state (or the United States for that matter). I didn't change. People's perception of me changed.

If you're an Entrepreneur, you're the CEO, so make up your own title that communicates where you're going. Your self-worth determines your net-worth. By changing the way I introduced myself, I attracted more motivated Entrepreneurs to my team. People perceived me to be more successful, and wanted to do business with me. Perception became reality.

You're reading this book, so you already have a million-dollar vision to develop your business locally, regionally, nationwide, or worldwide (even if you don't know it). Introduce yourself as "that" person. Because, you are! Meaning: dress and introduce yourself as if your vision has already become a reality, so that you are perceived to be that person. Ray Kroc knew in his heart that the number on his sign would continue to go up. We all believed because he believed. You stand a little taller and straighter when the world can see what you see. Make your vision part of your "pitch." There's a Million $ Party Girl in all of us, waiting to rock our vision and have fun while we're doing it! People are visual, matching up what we see to what we hear. A Visionista better look like a Visionista. Perception will also vary from generation to generation. When I told my seventy-four-year-old dad the title of my book, he remarked (in his dad voice), "People will think you're a call girl." I responded with a big grin, "Sex sells!"

OK, so right about now you're having a conversation with yourself about putting your vision out there. Maybe you picked up the wrong book. What will your friends and family think? What if you fail (we'll get to that in the next chapter). How are you going to make *that* happen? Should you really put yourself out there like that? How will you find the time when you have a family that needs you? Remove your head for a minute, and think with your heart. Women are the "what if" Queens. We take the wind out of our own sails before we even get started.

Think of this: What if you built a million-dollar business? Change your "What if" I don't (fill in the blank) question to "What if" I do (fill in the blank). It's a simple change in mindset that can change your entire world.

Start by focusing on a past success. If you did it before, you can do it again. I never had success in direct selling; I had never sold candles, coached a team, developed Leaders, spoke in public, or built a million-dollar business. However, I did overcome a lot of obstacles to succeed in retail and corporate sales. I'm passionate about supporting women Entrepreneurs to achieve their big dreams. Look at me now, I'm writing a book! I didn't know I could do that either. What are your success stories, and what obstacles have you overcome? Play them over and over again to build the belief in yourself you need today. You can do this!

So, what if your vision builds a million-dollar business? Think of the abundance you will be creating. That's what really gets me fired up! It's not just about wealth for you, it's wealth for everyone you inspire, because you stepped out and created something BIGGER. Here's a simple example. Last year my team held 5,590 home parties—with more than 36,000 guests in attendance. Think about the impact on the economy and the abundance my vision created. That includes supermarkets that sold food that was served at the parties, lighters purchased to light the candles, purchases made with the income entrepreneurs earned, etc. It's a ripple that just keeps going! And that doesn't even count the number of UPS workers that delivered the products! You're welcome UPS!

Break out of your comfort zone and try something really "crazy," like telling someone about a dream that's been your best-kept secret. Whether it's getting up the courage to call someone you want to do business with, putting your vision out there for the world to see, or telling a family member you've found your passion, let your purpose be your guide. Grab some poster board and markers and start creating a vision that inspires others to act. When JFK announced his vision of putting a man on the moon, he had no idea how it was going to happen, but he inspired an entire nation to figure it out. That's how you know that you're on the right path—it should sound a little crazy.

A vision inspires, energizes, and motivates! Goals are the little steps that will take you there. Start with a map of the United States. Then, visualize your business growing in a specific state, region, or throughout the country, whichever is appropriate for your business model. Put a star (or whatever speaks to you) on the new areas you are developing, based on what makes the most sense. For example, my good friend and lawyer, Lynda Hinkle, branched out and opened offices in three counties (all within thirty minutes of each other) to make her vision of "a growing small firm that is a powerful advocate for its clients and also is an active participant in its community," a reality. She could have easily serviced clients from one office, but her vision guided her to expand to three.

Head out in the world and go where no woman has gone before! But don't go alone; being a solo-preneur can be very isolating. Team up with like-minded people and form a Mastermind group of women from different industries who can share their unique perspective, talent, and vision.

Napoleon Hill, author of *Think and Grow Rich* (*Chapter 3) introduced the concept of the Mastermind principle as "The coordination of knowledge and effort of two or more people, who work toward a definite purpose, in the spirit of harmony." Simply put, two (or ten) heads are better than one. I start my day with a Mastermind, walking three miles around a lake with my best friend and fellow Visionista, Robin. Creative thoughts flow as we walk and talk. We get inspiration from nature while we keep the middle-aged pounds off. It's exercise for our mind, soul, and body.

You can find or create a group by networking (see Resource Guide at the end of this book), joining Linkedin groups, Facebook/Twitter search, and web search. Mastermind with Leaders whose vision is in line with yours and who will be committed to showing up. Mastermind groups are for the "will be's," not the "wannabes." Women love to socialize and connect, so include at least fifteen minutes in the beginning of your Mastermind meeting for mix and mingle. When it's time to get down to business, go around the room and ask each person to address any issues or opportunities. Allow time for discussion and feedback. I recommend that you pick someone to lead the discussion, and delegate a timekeeper.

Create a community of Visionistas who support each other with respect, integrity, and a passion to live an abundant life.

NOTES:

CREATE A VISION STATEMENT – WHO

WILL YOU SHARE IT WITH?

Secret #6
Failure Is Your Blessing

"Success is often achieved by those who don't know that failure is inevitable."
—Coco Chanel

"WHAT WOULD YOU do if you knew you couldn't fail?" That's a common motivational quote. And it's wrong. Failure is necessary to succeed and will become your biggest blessing.

As children, we're encouraged to fail from our very first step. When we fall down, our mom claps to show her enthusiasm, and we're encouraged to try again. We get a standing ovation for failing. Somewhere between our baby steps and adulthood we become conditioned to the idea that failure is bad. No parent or teacher is going to clap when you bring home a paper with an "F." The reality is that you have to fail to succeed. You have to fail *a lot*. It's time to liberate yourself from the F word. Failing is good. It means you're trying new things and figuring out what doesn't work—so you can do things that do work. Failure gives you courage to face new challenges and builds your character. The reason I built a million-dollar business wasn't because I was more successful. It's because I failed more times than most people, and I kept going.

After three years in business, I could see my dream in sight, developing a highly productive Leadership team that was on its way to reaching one million in annual revenue. I was asked to speak at Regional and National Conferences. Everyone wanted to know what we were doing. I was coaching women who were Visionistas in their own right, like Bunny, a single mom of two boys who started her business to pay for Christmas and was planning on quitting after the holidays. Instead of quitting, she became one of the top Leaders in the nation, celebrating twenty years as a Million $ Party Girl this July. There was also Holly, a twenty-something, single girl who started her business to pay off some bills. Over the course of her business, Holly got married, had three babies, left the business when family life got busy, and came back last year to start anew. In one month, she was Leading a Team, it's who she is. This year, both Bunny and Holly were there to see my daughter, the five-year-old they met twenty years ago, walk up the aisle at her wedding. My story about overcoming failure is really the shared stories of hundreds of incredible women I've met along my journey. Robin, Carol, Terry, Sarah, Carolyn, Faye, Sharon, Kara, Tracy, Tammy, Kris the list goes on. We've experienced happy, joyful times together, as well as challenging, tearful, frustrating, ready-to-throw-in-the-towel times. I didn't know it, but my "throw-in-the-towel-time" was about to happen.

I was awarded with an honorary "Regional Vice President (RVP)" title, and our team planned a big party with family and friends to celebrate our success. Every RVP had a team name, so Bill and I sat down to brainstorm ours. After a few hours of listing words that inspired us, we came up with Solid Gold. The gold standard was considered to be the best in the world, and you could hear the word "goal" in Gold. Solid meant we had a strong foundation. It had a nice ring to it. I was off to buy a gold dress to wear to the party (it's all about the dress) and felt like a bride at her wedding. Lauren and Alyssa were invited and got special dresses, too. They were awarded a stuffed animal from a home office VP and got to see firsthand what happens when you reach for your dreams. Both my girls fell asleep under a table on my mom's faux fur coat as our team celebrated our achievement.

Within three months of the celebration party, our team started to unravel. Like a loose thread, we were coming apart at the seams. A well-respected key Leader had to quit to take care of a sick relative. Her best friend, who was also part of our Leader team, soon followed. A few months later another key Leader had to stop working due to personal problems. My team was falling like dominoes, and there was nothing I could do to stop it. The momentum that created our team in three years destroyed it within one year. The party was over.

The Visionista in me started to let the trash-talking Doubter into the conversation. How could everything I worked so hard to build be taken away so quickly? What was the point of three years of effort? My family was right—this business won't work. I felt like a complete failure. I thought I'd finally be able to exceed my previous corporate income, and now I had to start all over. That alarm had already rung, and I was out of time. Maybe my mother was right; I should have been a teacher. Bill started to leave the help wanted ads out for me, as his patience was growing thin. I promised him I could make this business work and we'd have a better life for our family. Instead, we were faced with an uncertain future. I always thought failure was the opposite of success, never considering I could succeed and then fail.

I began to play that blame game I talked about. It was everyone's fault but mine. Whining that my business failed because I had no control over other people's decisions and actions (forgetting that I could control my own) became my favorite past time. I escaped into my bubble of a self-imposed pity party and stopped reaching out to my mentors. They might see the big L (Loser) on my forehead. When I look at pictures of myself from that year, I don't even recognize myself. Feeling sorry for yourself is not attractive. There was no joy or glow radiating from my face. I looked sick. Turns out I had come down with a common failure malady, Poor Little Old Me (PLOM) disease. It's a semi-chronic affliction. I hid out in my self-proclaimed Loserville, afraid it might be contagious. Hanging out with other PLOM patients prolongs the disease. If you get this disease, recognize these symptoms early so you can get treatment. My PLOM pity party went on for a year. It was more of a festival, without the guacamole and margaritas.

At the same time, Bill found out he was losing his job as part of a corporate layoff. Just kick me while I'm down. We considered selling the house, and we cut back our expenses to the bare minimum. Working for someone else was the only way out of our situation. So, I got a sales job and went back to work, still maintaining my business on a part-time basis. I was so absorbed in my own problems that I barely had time to focus on Alyssa, who was having learning problems in kindergarten. When she got tested for first grade, they discovered she could only recognize five letters of the alphabet. How could I not know that? Failing as a mother brought me back to reality. It was time to snap out of it and wake up. Enough already! I went into work that day and gave my notice, not caring what happened to my financial future. My daughter had twenty-one letters of the alphabet to learn. Bill landed on his feet, getting a job with a new company sooner, rather than later. We were all looking forward to a new beginning. Somehow, we would make it all work.

After a long look in the mirror, I took responsibility for my business, and my life. It wasn't the choices my team made; it was the choices I made. It's OK to celebrate success, but I celebrated and then stopped doing what I did to get there in the first place. I thought success was in the "arrival." The truth is we never arrive. I had fallen into the big trap, putting all my expectations and self-worth into achieving a specific result. When the result was different from what I planned on, I became paralyzed, unable to move forward. My belief and self-worth quickly deteriorated. Why didn't Spencer Johnson write *Who Moved My Cheese* a few years earlier?

I refocused on my purpose and passion, reminding myself of the reasons I started my business in the first place. It was never about the money. My passion was to share my glow and empower women to discover theirs—that's what gives me joy. I reconnected with my mentors – Gail and Denise - who never stopped believing in me. Instead of hiding out, I started to attend seminars and conferences again. If only I had done this a year ago, I'd have saved myself a lot of angst and rebuilt my business a whole lot faster. But, we can never look back. I needed to learn those lessons so I could be a better coach, mentor, and Leader.

At first, I was concerned about what my peers would think of me, but a surprising thing happened. They didn't judge me on my failure. They judged me on how I had impacted their life. One by one, people came up and told me stories of something I had said while speaking at a conference or of a goal I achieved that inspired them to succeed. All this time I was wallowing in self-pity, not even considering something I said or did might have touched someone's life. It was so selfish of me. I needed to get out of my own way and focus my efforts on serving women. To rebuild my confidence and self-esteem, I set and achieved monthly goals, starting over from the bottom, one baby step at a time. It didn't take long for me to get fired up about the business again. I was doing what I loved, building people. Within two years I rebuilt my Leadership team, and we generated our first million dollars in revenue. I was back!

Here are the blessings that failure taught me. Whatever the world wants to throw at me now, I'm ready!

Beware of the Big Trap. Your self-worth is not based on one outcome. The outcome might have changed, but what you've achieved has not. No one can erase that. Pick yourself up, take control, and focus on your past success. If you did it before, you can do it again. Take time to evaluate so you can adjust your settings: What did you do that worked? What do you need to change?

Success Is a Journey, Don't Forget Your GPS. Whenever I've failed in business, my friends and mentors would try to comfort me with this familiar quote, "Success is a journey, not a destination." What people forget to tell you is that you need to bring your GPS, or who knows where your journey will take you. I'd never get in the car without my GPS charged and a Google map backup (just in case the sexy Australian voice coming out of my GPS is wrong). I mistakenly thought when I reached my destination, the journey was over. My "I've arrived" attitude made me complacent, and I stopped setting an intention for where I wanted my business to go next. Having a new goal or dream to reach for never occurred to me. Forward motion set with intention propels our opportunity and keeps us focused on the road ahead. There will always be detours, but if we are driving with intention, the detour will most likely come from inspired action. Act on inspiration, and take the detour. It will always "recalculate" you and point you on the road to opportunity.

Anticipate, Don't React. My mother used to say, "Don't put all your eggs in one basket." I did exactly the opposite and was caught off guard when my business fell apart, leaping into reaction mode. It's kind of like swimming upstream against a strong current—exhausting. Successful Entrepreneurs are always thinking about what their next big deal or client will be. They don't put all their eggs in one basket. Failure taught me that what's here today, may be gone tomorrow, so don't stop working. Celebrate your success, have a good night's sleep, and wake up with a what's next attitude. Then get back to work.

The Best Things in Life Are Free, or on Sale. I've gone back and forth from rags to riches more times than I can count. Whether I shop at Target or Nordstrom, does it really matter? It's your attitude in the dress that makes you look like a million bucks. A Million $ Party Girl makes the most of what she has. Thanks to failure, I discovered TJ Maxx. That's a blessing! I learned that life experiences are more important than labels. I've been to live shows such as *The View*, *The Daily Show*, and *The Late Show With David Letterman*—all FREE. I seem to attract interesting people and interesting places, also all free.

Stop Trying. What do we say when a girlfriend asks us to lunch and we don't want go? I'll try. We both know that we have no intention of going. Trying is planning to fail. It sends a message to your brain that you can't or won't do it. To quote Yoda,

"DO, or Do not. There is no try." You might fail, but you still did it, and if it didn't work, you'll do something else. When I had PLOM disease, I used failure words like try, can't, hope, and wish as my excuses. I told my friends, "I tried, but it just didn't work" or "I'm hoping to get my business back." I recognize it instantly now. When someone tells me they are trying to achieve a goal, earn an incentive trip, or attend a success conference, I know they have no intention of doing it.

Get out of your bubble. Even though you're not feeling like you want to see anybody, get dressed, and get out the door. Make your mess your success, and share your story. Connect with your mentor, coach, and fellow Visionistas. Chances are, they've been where you are and can offer you support and advice. Volunteer and get involved in your community. If you want to put perspective on your life, serve meals at a soup kitchen. Being thankful brings you to the present moment. I wake up every day grateful I can get out of bed and put my two feet on the floor. That's a blessing.

NOTES:

WHAT HAVE YOUR FAILURES

TAUGHT YOU?

Secret #7
Girls Really Do Just Want to Have Fun

"You grow up the day you have your first real laugh at yourself."
—Ethel Barrymore

A S ONE OF the few women in direct selling to come from a corporate background in the early 1990s, I brought a unique perspective to the business. I was used to being the odd man out, so to speak. Men do business differently than women, wanting to get right to the facts, cut to the chase, and close the deal. Women are emotional, we want to talk about our new shoes and find out how the kids are doing. In my corporate job, I could never let my inner party girl come out. Other than wearing my favorite hot pink suit, I still had to speak with authority and leave my "girlyness" at the door. Instead of talking "girl talk" with my male clients, I'd compliment them on the framed achievements that were proudly displayed on their walls. Men like to talk about their "wall of fame."

Switching gears over to a world that was ninety-nine percent businesswomen was a culture shock for me. At my first sales meeting, they were awarding Miss America–looking sashes and tiaras to the top sales women. I thought they had to be joking. What did I get myself into? I was a successful businesswoman with brains and skills, not a beauty queen. There was no way I was wearing a sash. I shared my "Miss America" concerns with the women that led the team. If we were going to attract more corporate businesswomen like me, we needed to take our sales meetings into the next century, which was just ten years away. With an open-minded attitude, they embraced my ideas and agreed that it was time for a change.

Recognition was an unknown to me, so I had to adapt to this new "cheerleader-like" environment. In my sales job, my paycheck was considered to be my recognition for a job well done. The corporate world is not known for giving pats on the back.

I discovered that the cheering and pats on the back felt pretty good. I was never picked for cheerleading in high school, so maybe this was my chance for revenge. Girls really do just want to have fun, including me. I started to let down my guard, and embraced the concept that success didn't have to be so serious. Maybe the boys were wrong. Get me my tiara.

We brainstormed recognition ideas, looking to come up with something that was fun, but more appropriate for modern-day women. Our team decided on ribbons, a smaller more 1990s version of the Miss America sash. Ribbons are fun, reminding us of our youth when we won sporting events or spelling bees. We had ribbons in every color for every level of achievement. If you made progress, got results, were in the tops, had a great attitude, you name it, you got a ribbon! The more ribbons we gave, the more we built our team's self-confidence. A top achiever's goal was to look like a peacock at our sales meeting, with a "fan" of colored ribbons hanging from her nametag. Have you ever heard the saying, proud as a peacock? Males have been strutting their stuff for years; it's time women did, too. If only we had Facebook back then, we could have taken a picture of the peacock-looking ribbons and put it on everyone's Facebook wall. Then all their friends would know that they were a peacock, too.

Our new form of recognizing success taught me that recognition isn't about the dollar value of the gift or prize, it's about how you make people feel. A sincere word of praise and a bright-colored ribbon that is given from the heart in front of your peers is priceless. We started out with custom-printed ribbons but found even more fun styles at the dollar store. They had an entire display of ribbons for teachers, with all kinds of sayings we could use for our business, including Great Effort, Super Star, and Excellent! Our sales team loved it! We continued to build on fun ideas, discovering that we're all just kids at heart who want to be praised for a job well done. We used sombreros to recognize our Mexico trip achievers, feather boas for "Bonus Babes" (top sales people who earned bonuses), 100 Grand candy bars for Entrepreneurs who were building teams, raffle tickets for fun prize bag drawings—you get the idea. I don't know who was having more fun, me when I gave out the recognition, or the people I was recognizing.

We knew we were onto something, and took this concept to our parties, using fun recognition incentives like early bird, bringing a party crasher, or pre-booking a party. The party crasher idea was not mine; we heard it from another Leader who got her inspiration after watching the movie, *Wedding Crashers*. Recognizing party crashers was really fun, since being a "crasher" was not something you were usually encouraged to do. Party Crashers didn't know the Hostess so they were new Customers that we normally wouldn't get a chance to meet. The more crashers we had, the more our Customer base grew. Wouldn't you love to have new Customers "crash" your business?

Recognizing a larger group of people; those who made progress, gave an effort and generated results (instead of just the same top three people all the time) was a big lesson in Leadership for me. It taught me that you develop people by valuing their strengths, not by trying to fix their weakness. People have a whole lot more fun doing what they are good at. It builds their self-esteem and confidence to the point that it compensates for what they are not so good at. I embraced this concept and started to use a new coaching style called the 100/1 Rule; give 100% of your energy to the one thing you do really well. When a Sales Consultant, Kim, came to me and said she was ready to Lead a Team, it was the perfect time to give the 100/1 Rule a test run, which was more fun for me, too. My style is to build people up and empower them to figure out the "how" themselves. When you believe in people, they will show you that they are capable of amazing things!

Kim's "numbers" showed me that she hadn't quite mastered the skills of a Sales Consultant. Her weakness was consistency in her business. The one thing she loved to do was creative product displays. She also participated in and attended all our training workshops and was an asset to the team. Kim also was fun, lighting up the room with her positive energy, and she had one of the traits I value most in a Leader, an attitude of gratitude. Kim would be a great Leader if she could be more consistent with her business. Instead of going on about what she needed to do to build a more consistent business, I congratulated her on her strengths and put her in charge of creating a product display, as well as training at our regional meeting. She would be showcasing her talents in front of 100 women. Kim was in her element. Every person in that room was taking notes, writing down Kim's creative ideas, including me. I was in awe of the person she blossomed into, right before my eyes. After the event, Kim received kudos and praise from everyone in the room. She was the star of the show. By the next day, she called to tell me she had doubled the amount of parties on her calendar. She had known what she needed to do to build her business all along. Once Kim built up her belief system, she was able to make it happen. Within two months, she was Leading a Team. Enthusiasm on fire!

"Girls Just Want To Have Fun" became my motto for everything I did. After all, if I didn't think an idea was fun and exciting, how could I convince anyone else that it was? People are happy when they are having fun. Happy people love what they do and attract abundance to their business. It's what I call the fun factor.

I adapted this concept to team-building as well, creating themed training events, weekend Leader Retreats at the shore, and limo rides into the city. At our holiday parties, we push back the furniture and make room for dancing and karaoke. After our Regional events, Leaders go out for "After Happy Hour, Happy Hour." Recently, we went to a bar that had a Quizzo's game going on. There were six of us, so the DJ named our Quizzo's Team "12 Boobs and a Candle," which provided us with unlimited laughter all night long. When our annual incentive trip was to the Hard Rock Hotel, I created a four-month "School of Rock" training program, complete with blow up guitars. The Solid Gold team knows how to rock! The "graduation" for top achievers was a limo bus ride to New York City for the day, which included lunch, a "photo op" at the Hard Rock Times Square, touring Midtown, and a visit to the 911 Memorial.

Fun is a part of my presentations, too. During a speech about vision, I wore huge clown sunglasses and handed out dollar store kiddie sunglasses to the attendees, letting them know their future was so bright, they needed to wear shades. I'm certainly no comedian, but I do like to crack myself up. I've learned to not take myself so seriously, especially as I get older. Why can't work, shopping, learning, even the news be more fun? I recently switched to watching *Good Morning America* for the simple reason that the *Good Morning America* crew looked like they were having more fun. I'd rather start my day with fun people.

As time went on, and we entered the twenty-first century, the old ways of training my team were no longer relevant. Increasing gas prices and over-scheduled moms all contributed to the decline in attendance. I needed to discover new innovative ideas to connect and engage with my sales team and Leaders. We had moved into the information age, with instant access to anything and everything we wanted to know. Waiting a month to learn how to build your business at a seminar that you had to drive to seemed obsolete. To get someone (anyone) to leave their home and show up for a meeting, you'd better be doing something really fun, and that starts with not calling it a meeting or a workshop. The recession was also looming, and I needed new, fun ways to engage and connect with our Customers – providing value and loyalty.

I needed to clear my head and go for a walk with my Mastermind walking partner, Robin. We walked, we talked, and we brainstormed innovative ideas that would provide a solution to both problems—connecting with our sales team and our

Customers. After walking three miles, we had an outline (in our heads) for a new type of meeting, an experience. We would call it an event, which in itself sounded more fun and exciting. People want to go to events; they don't want to go to meetings and workshops. Our event concept was a fun and interactive experience. We got rid of the podium, where our speakers normally presented, and got out into the audience, involving both Consultants and Customers. They loved our products, so why not let them tell us what they were excited about. If something on the agenda wasn't guest-friendly—meaning it didn't engage Customers—we didn't do it. In fact, we got rid of most of our agenda and focused on more mix, mingle, and fun.

We called our spring product launch, Step Into Spring. It included a "Fashion Shoe" contest (which had nothing to do with candles but was a whole lot of fun), wine bar, chocolate tasting, mini-facials, angel card readings, and more. In addition to beautiful product displays that showcased our new products, we supported local women biz owners by inviting them to showcase their products. Our Customers got a style makeover and "modeled" our new products on the runway, as the founder of the Shoe Society, Cristina Candullo, judged Best in Shoe. We also invited a local photographer, Danielle DiAngelo of AngelEye Photography, to take pictures and promote her business. The event was a huge success.

When people are having fun, they are motivated to act. It's that "Enthusiasm on fire is better than knowledge on ice" thing. Wine helps, too. Our sales team was generating results, while Customers purchased product, booked parties, and joined our team. I transitioned my training programs to weekly teleconference and webcasts, bringing the information directly to the

Entrepreneur on their time, when they wanted to learn it. Since all my programs are recorded, moms can listen after the kids go to bed, and full-time workers can tune in during their lunch break. The Regional Meetings of five years ago now seem like ancient history.

When was the last time you got really excited about your business? Innovating, creating, and transforming will inspire your Fun Factor. I'm having a blast embracing technology along my success journey, which provides more opportunities for me to live my purpose and serve women. Most of the time I have no idea how I do what I do—I just keep clicking. I blog, pin, tweet, Facebook, YouTube, teleconference, and webcast. Recently, I was the Guest Radio Co-Host of Girl Talk with Host Whitney Ullman. Whitney set the tone ahead of time that her show was about "nourishing your inner Diva." Diva is like Visionista; they're both fun words. Cyndi Lauper said it best, with one lyric change, "When the working day is *begun*, Girls—they want to have fun."

NOTES:

WHAT IS YOUR FUN FACTOR?

Secret #8
Hard Work Will Not Make You Successful

"I love to see a young girl go out and grab the world by the lapels. Life's a bitch. You've got to go out and kick ass."
—Maya Angelou

CONTRARY TO WHAT you've heard, hard work is not the key to success—unless you're working hard on the right things.

Vision + Intention + Inspired Action + Numbers = RESULTS

You can be busy all day "working," but if you don't have an intention that is focused on achieving your vision, the only goal you'll accomplish is frustration. It may feel good to be busy all day, but after weeks and months of busy activities you'll find that your business is going nowhere. You can't figure out why because, after all, you've been working hard for months (maybe years). It's time to get off the gerbil wheel.

Once you've defined your Vision, set an Intention. An Intention is a declaration that moves you in the direction of your dream or goal. I could easily spend all day organizing my office, wrapping up prizes for events, or playing Farmville. None of those things serve my intention. My office will probably never be organized, but thanks to paperless technology I don't need to keep piles of paper or business cards anymore. There's an App for that. "Busy things" can be delegated to kids, part-time assistants, high school students looking for part-time work, or even your mom. Get your family involved in making your vision a reality. When Lauren and Alyssa were kids, they became very good at wrapping door prizes for my events.

My vision to serve a gazillion women by sharing my glow, and empowering women to discover theirs, guides my daily intention. It can be as simple as making someone's day by sharing a smile, giving away free tealights without expecting a return, or making time to volunteer at a food bank. My intention guided me to write this book. I've written hundreds of speeches over the last twenty-two years as a speaker, but I've never written a book. I set an intention, and my mind responded with the inspired action to write a book. I simply listened and followed my gut, never challenging whether it was possible. The typical negative self-talk conversation of "Who am I to think I can write a book, and why would anyone want to read it?" never came up. Although, I did hear from the villains that the thought had crossed their minds. They must have forgotten I have a golden lasso. Who am I? I am woman.

"I Am Woman," was the first song Helen Reddy ever wrote. The story goes that her record label asked her to write one final song for her album. Helen had no idea how she was going to do it; she had never written lyrics. But before she went to bed, she sent an intention to write a song that empowered women. According to Wikipedia, Helen is quoted as saying, "I couldn't find any songs that said what I thought being a woman was about. I thought about these strong women in my family who had gotten through the Depression and world wars and drunken, abusive husbands. But there was nothing in music that reflected that. . . . I never thought of myself as a songwriter, but it came down to having to do it." She continued, "I remember lying in bed one night and the words, 'I am strong, I am invincible, I am woman,' kept going over and over in my head. That part I consider to be divinely inspired. I had been chosen to get a message across." Pressed on who had chosen her, she replied, "The universe." Forty years later, Kathryn Bigelow became the first woman Director to win an Oscar. The orchestra played "I Am Woman" as she finished her acceptance speech. Helen Reddy's intention and inspired action left the world a legacy.

When you set a daily intention, you are sending a request to your subconscious mind, which responds with inspired action. Tune in! Inspired action feels easy and effortless; there's no doubt because you know in your gut it's what you're supposed to be doing. Inspiration comes to me when I can free my mind and just BE. For me, it's usually when I am just waking up and setting my intention for the day, or when I'm in the shower, driving, or during my morning "Mastermind walk" with Robin. Inspired action starts flowing and moves me in the direction of my dreams.

When I first started my business, Bill and I were just getting settled into a new home and community. Because I was working full-time, there was no time to get to know my neighbors or join community groups. Like many busy working parents, we worked all day and pulled into our driveway with the "disappearing reflex." In one click, the garage door magically opened and we pulled right in, instantly closing the door to the outside world behind us. How on earth would I build my business when I had few local friends or connections? I had no idea. After setting an intention to connect with people who wanted what I had to offer, I woke with an inspired action. My gut told me to go to the women's gyms in the area and share my glow. I had to get to where the women were. I threw some catalogs and tealights in my tote and was on my way. The worst that could happen is I would make someone's day by giving them a free gift.

In the 1990s, women embraced aerobics and a new kind of workout called, Step Class. Walking into the aerobic studio, I was greeted by a friendly woman behind the counter, Dawn. She didn't seem like she would bite. I didn't have a pre-rehearsed pitch; my inspiration had just arrived an hour earlier, so there was not much time to plan. I simply introduced myself with a big smile and asked if she liked candles. Corporate sales taught me that it's important to find out if a prospect wants or needs your product before you launch into your sales pitch. Thankfully, she did! In fact, Dawn was very excited to meet me. She had a pet and wanted her home to smell more welcoming than essence of stinky dog. I thanked her for being so welcoming and gave her a tealight as a gift. Give and you will receive. Dawn asked if she could see a catalog (I just happened to have one!) and ordered one of our biggest candles, a six-by-eight-inch, three-wick (I call it the Mother of all Candles), on the spot. I liked Dawn so much I joined the gym.

Dawn and I started brainstorming how we could help each other. She wanted to add value to her client's membership, and I needed to find new Customers. People can't help you if you don't ask for what you need. Inspired action answered the call, and I offered to donate a gift basket for a client appreciation drawing. We set up the basket on the counter with a pile of door prize slips and a fishbowl—very low tech. Dawn picked the busiest aerobics' class to pick the winner, live. She even let me set up a product display so that I could show off more of my candles and home decor. We were like-minded women helping women. My inspired action changed my business. I booked six new parties with women who loved candles and loved to entertain. There were my ideal clients, "Demo Divas." The fishbowl was full of names and phone numbers (we didn't have e-mail yet), also known as leads.

Giving away a free candle attracted a welcoming response from Dawn, so I continued to give. I called all the leads and told them they won...a new fragrance! Because they were all local, I had the opportunity to drop off their new fragrance and build a relationship, asking what type of fragrances they liked and where they used candles in their home. Many of those women became close friends. I found a direct result between meeting new Customers and how quickly my business expanded. It made sense. Out of the 100 Leads, I generated eleven new parties. My corporate sales background kicked in, and I started to calculate my "closing rate." How many people would I need to talk to, to find my ideal client, and make my Million $ Party Girl Vision a reality? Everything in life can break down to a mathematical equation.

Start your day with intention, act on inspiration, generate the right numbers, and you'll be on your way to achieving your goals and dreams. Keep in mind that the numbers only matter if you're getting in front of your ideal client. Many sales managers track success by how many calls you make, forgetting that those calls may be a waste of time if the client doesn't need what you have to offer. That's like me getting a sales booth at the Fragrance Allergy Convention, probably not such a good idea. Or, as my mom would say, "You're barking up the wrong tree."

If you're not there yet, most likely you are not generating the numbers you need to get a YES. Break it down to all aspects of your business. For example, if you know your average sale, you can do two things to achieve your sales goals: (1) increase your sale average by serving your Customer better and (2) increase the number of Customers you sell to. I knew if I had a party with a "Demo Diva" she'd have ten to twenty people attend. Divas are experts at "generating the numbers" (more guests and sales) because they know we are business partners. They're earning a free shopping spree, and I'm earning a profit. If I booked a party with someone who was hosting it just to help me out, I'd be lucky to have five people attend. Her intention was helping me; she didn't really care about the rest. It takes me the same time to speak to an audience of 10 or 1,000 people. A larger audience equals larger results. The same principle can be applied to corporate clients. It took me the same amount of time and effort to close a deal with a small client as it did a Fortune 500 company; therefore I focused on the Fortune 500 companies. Know your numbers.

Twenty-two years later, I'm still making new connections and adding Social Media to build relationships. According to the 2011 U.S. Census Bureau, 311,591,917 live in the United States. Determine how many are your ideal client, and get to work.

Here are my top tips for making new connections:

1. **Sampling**. Whether you sell a product or a service, you have samples. For example, I can give a free tea-light (product) or a video of me speaking (service). Give with no expectation of gain. It's good Karma, baby. You never know when it will come back to you, times ten. Don't give a sample without getting a name, cell phone number, or e-mail address so you can follow up. I like e-mail addresses because I connect with them on Face-book, which in my business, builds a relationship. Let them know you want to get feedback about your product or service and ask what the best way is to connect: text, Facebook, e-mail, phone, or tweet?

2. **Vendor Events/Expos**. These are both great ways to get out and make new connections, as long as they are attracting attendees that are your ideal client. Give your table the Fun Factor! Create an interactive display that draws people in. The biggest mistake Entrepreneurs make is that they don't follow up. Make personal notes on your lead slips so that your follow-up is genuine—and connect with everyone you meet. Even if they don't need your product or service, they might know someone who does. When I sold printing, the vendor that had the biggest crowd at an Expo was giving away chocolate. Chocolate makes people happy. Stand in front of your table or booth and engage attendees with a fun giveaway or a contest/prize drawing. One of our Leaders, Michelle, fills a hurricane jar with M & M's and gives a prize to the person who can guess how many M & M's are in the hurricane.

Her table always draws a big crowd. To be in the drawing, participants fill out a quick survey that includes their contact information. Make your display attractive by using what I call "Triangle Marketing." Display your visuals, products, and props in a triangle, using height to raise items on the top of the triangle. Phone books and catering trays are free risers that can be easily found at most events. I've even used a pot. Cover your risers with fabric or tablecloth so no one will know your secret. An eight-foot table should have three triangles.

3. **Referrals.** What is the value of a new Customer to you? Offer incentives to your existing Customers that create a constant flow of new Customers knocking on your door. Social Media is a great tool for your Customers to share your business with all the people they know, for free. We love to tell the world what we're doing, where we're going, and what our favorite products are. Within two weeks of creating the Million $ Party Girl Facebook page (facebook.com/milliondollarpartygirl) I had 213 Likes that reached 2,564 people. My 213 fans have 94,961 friends. You can't afford to not be on Pinterest, Twitter, Linkedin, and YouTube. Blogging will also build your following and Search Engine Optimization (SEO), sending referrals your way.

4. **Client Retention.** Create a Customer loyalty program. Supermarkets and pharmacies led the way by getting us all to sign up for a loyalty card that gives us an incentive to come back and shop again. Pizza shops also use a loyalty program; buy ten, get one FREE! How can *you* reward your customers to keep them coming back?

5. **Speaking.** If you're the best-kept secret in your field—get out and speak. Share your expertise with networking groups, community associations, chambers of commerce, Mastermind groups, and industry or trade associations. Be prepared with an offer so that your speaking leads to new connections and business. Build your audience before and after you speak by sharing a free video, blog, or engaging in a discussion on Linkedin or Facebook.

6. **Networking.** Networking, or what I call Consciously Connecting, is key to building your business. You can do all the points I listed above while networking. Three things to remember when making new connections: (1) focus on what you can do for them, not what they can do for you; (2) most people you meet don't know what to say either (use positive body language to send out a message that you are approachable); and (3) follow your gut and follow up. I can sense who is a like-minded Visionista. That's whom I'm meeting up with for coffee after the event. If you're new to networking, refer to the Women's Networking Resource Guide at the end of this book to get started. Chances are you'll be able to attend an event this week.

NOTES:

WHAT IS YOUR INTENTION?

Secret #9
Persistence Does Not Always Mean Pushy

"The quickest way to know a woman is to go shopping with her."
—Marcelene Cox

EVERYONE IS IN sales. Doctors sell, lawyers sell, colleges sell, and your hairdresser sells. Has your mom ever convinced you to do something you didn't want to do? Yeah, she was selling, too. Women are natural sellers. We talked our husband into that family vacation when our kids were in high school because, "It's the last time our kids will ever want to vacation with us!" (Trust me, your kids will never say no to a free vacation). Or, when my children were young, I used this nugget, "We're making childhood memories that will last forever!" Do you remember anything before the age of five? Probably not, but we can convince our husband that we need to spend $5,000 because our three-year-old will remember the trip to Disney *forever*. You closed the deal by focusing on the outcome, and created a sense of urgency with a deadline. Now do that for your business.

Why do women love to shop, but we're afraid to ask people to buy? We're so good at selling other people's things, such as calling our girlfriends and telling all our Facebook friends about a great book (like this one, hint hint), restaurant, or a sale. When it comes to our own business, we hold back, or even end the sale before the Customer is done shopping. Fear takes over, controlling our thoughts about money, rejection, and success. Lack of money, belief, and security—there's a lot a lot of crap going on between our ears. Anxiety about debt is a huge limiter. If you don't think you can afford what you're offering, or don't see the value in it, you'll subconsciously stop your Customer from purchasing it.

If I had a nickel for every time I heard the "I don't want to be pushy" excuse, I would be the Billion $ Party Girl. The sheer fact that you're worried about being pushy should tell you, you never would be. It's not in your DNA. Pushy people don't worry about being pushy and will never have long-term success because they are not serving their Customer's needs. They serve themselves. Focus on serving others by solving problems. Then you'll stop worrying that you're being pushy, which is really about that scary two-letter word, N-O. We don't take rejection well. It's no wonder; we spent most of our youth trying to be liked by the popular crowd and get a date to the prom.

What if you changed your mindset about the word No, embracing your differences and becoming BFFs? Yolanda Yes is a great girlfriend, but your fear of Natalie No is keeping you from meeting more Yolandas, and making more sales. Natalie is not saying No to being your friend. She really likes you. She's saying No to what you're serving for dinner. You see, she's a vegan, and you're serving up steak. It's not for her, but you wouldn't have known that if you didn't offer her a steak. That's OK—we can all live on this planet together, vegans and steak eaters alike.

By reaching out to more Natalies, you end up making friends with more Yolandas. Soon your contact list is full of more friends and Customers than you ever imagined.

About five years into my business, our Leader Team brainstormed ideas to overcome the "No" obstacle. It got in the way of many of our sales reps' success because they were afraid to offer our products and services for fear of being perceived as pushy, and hearing the word No. Can you relate? Our solution was to invite Natalie No to the party. We called it the "100 NO Challenge." Bring it on! At our sales meeting, each Consultant received a chart with three columns (Name, Contact Info, and the Reason for the No) and 100 rows. The challenge was to fill the chart; thereby getting 100 No's. We knew that if they got 100 No's, they would also get many more Yes's. The challenge worked and increased our sales by twenty percent. It was a big eye opener for all of us. Not only did our sales team generate more business, they turned many No's into opportunities because they found out the reason for the No. That in turn, built their confidence and helped them overcome their fear of No.

You can't solve a problem if you don't know what it is. For example, if someone said No to booking a party, the typical response was, "Thanks anyway." Then we'd hang up and stop making calls because we felt so rejected. Instead, the sales rep asked, "Do you mind if I ask why?" A common answer was "I don't think I know enough people." They actually wanted to have a party, but had their own fear of rejection (feeling exactly like we did). That was a problem we could solve. We offered to help them create a list of neighbors, friends, family, and coworkers. Turns out they knew a whole lot more people than they thought they did. The No became a Yes!

I recently attended a home party to mentor a new Consultant, modeling for her how to serve each Customer's needs. One particular Customer was very excited about a new collection to decorate her home. I suggested she host a party to get it all free, but that was not her thing. She wanted to shop. I asked what areas she wanted to decorate, listened to her response, and discovered that she hated her empty tables and walls. She said her house felt gloomy. That's a problem I can solve. I focused on the outcome, transforming her home from gloomy to "glowy." When she finally found the last item she needed, the order totaled in the hundreds. I continued to serve, making sure she had the right candle for each accessory she purchased. I happily totaled the order for her, not because I just made a big sale for a new Consultant, but because I saw how thrilled the Customer was with all the help and attention I gave her. She effortlessly handed over a check with a big Thank YOU! The new Consultant couldn't believe her eyes and asked how I got the Customer to spend so much money. I replied, "Simple, I solved her problem."

Self-sabotage is also a by-product of our fear of rejection. On a recent coaching call, my client shared that she was having a dry spell. Within weeks, her dry spell turned into a drought, attracting more cancellations and loss of business. She had the power to make it rain, yet she let her limits sabotage her business. Thoughts direct your actions, which direct your results.

STOP WORRYING ABOUT BEING PUSHY, START SERVING.

If you've been doing the cha cha dance, three steps forward and two steps back, take some time to do this exercise:

- Grab a piece of paper or notebook. Make four columns with these headings at the top: **Problem ~ Solution ~ Outcome ~ Offer.**
- Fill in the columns with common problems from your industry, along with your solution, outcome, and offer.

Here are some examples from my business to get your creative juices flowing.

Customer Problem	Solution	Outcome	Offer With a Limit
Home smells like a stinky dog.	Reed diffusers, electric warmer, and candles with a fresh, clean fragrance.	No longer embarrassed to invite friends over. You love your dog and your home, again.	Buy a reed diffuser with three dozen tealights and get an electric warmer at half price. Sale ends ____.
Job loss or experienced a pay cut.	Earn a free Starter Kit and start a home party or online business	Reduce your financial stress and replace your lost income, while having FUN.	Sign on bonus of an extra $____ ends ____.
Need client appreciation gifts for an upcoming event.	Personalized shopping experience to help you select the perfect gifts, at a great value.	Happy clients that remember you because you gave a unique gift = better client retention.	Buy ten, get three free. Offer ends ___.

The more you serve, the more you'll get out of your own way. Here's a wild thought, why limit your Customer's opportunity to buy from you? Leverage your talents to add extra streams of income. Just look at Visionistas, Bethenny Frankel and Jessica Simpson. They continue to serve their Customers by creating products they want. I can see Million $ Party Girl Glowtini's and Vision Wines in my future. Call me.

David Bach's book, *Start Late Finish Rich*, devotes an entire chapter to direct selling as one of the keys to achieving financial freedom. For example, if you're a masseuse, you can serve your clients needs by starting a business and offering aromatherapy soy candles. Find something that stays true to your passion, vision, and your brand. Open your mind to all the possibilities that are available to you. I've built a multimillion-dollar business, but that doesn't mean I'm ready to lie down and take a nap. I'm just getting started, expanding my business to include writing, speaking, blogging, and webcasts so that I can serve more women. Join Team Visionistas, like-minded women who take risks and break from the crowd.

NOTES:

WHAT PROBLEM DOES YOUR PROD-
UCT OR SERVICE SOLVE?

HOW DOES IT MAKE PEOPLE FEEL?

Secret #10
Your Business Is Your Life

"No one ever died from sleeping in an unmade bed."
—Erma Bombeck

I HAVE A CONFESSION to make, I'm not perfect. My beds are not always made, and sometimes my husband eats cereal for dinner. Visionistas may have super powers, but we can't do it all. Don't sweat the small stuff. I frequently reminded my family "There are people starving in Africa," as I poured the Cheerios out of the box. Juggling a full-time job, home, kids, and a husband was exhausting, even when I had a nanny. There was still dinner to make, laundry to do, and bedtime stories to read. Most of the time I felt like one of those zombies walking around in *The Night of the Living Dead*. (Although, they probably got more sleep than me.) When I quit my corporate job, my head was filled with dreams of baking homemade cookies with my children while simultaneously running my candle empire. Of course, that dream-stuff only happens in the movies. My daughters, Lauren and Alyssa, will tell you that the only cookies we made were slice and bake ones. And they probably did the slicing and baking.

We frequently hear the message that it's your business on one side, and your life on the other, and that we need to balance our life. I believe that's wrong. If you're passionate about what you're doing, your business IS your life, especially when your business is in your home. Inspired action might call me to jump in my office at anytime, night or day. When I get really excited about an idea, which is pretty often, I have to act on it. I learned early on that, as Hillary Clinton said, "It takes a village." Rather than feeling guilty about working, I included my children in my work. When they were three and five, they loved smelling all the candle fragrances and taking the wicks out of the votives—a great lesson in eye/hand coordination. It kept them busy for hours. As they got older, I empowered them to play and create product displays, using their unlimited childhood creativity. Their playroom was full of books, princess costumes, and art supplies. I never felt the need to entertain them; they could do that for themselves so much better than I could—acting out entire stories about make-believe worlds. Lauren (the big sister) was always the producer, giving Alyssa her "lines" and costume changes.

At age seven, I taught Alyssa how to explain our Leadership program, using a flip chart, fully believing that she could pull it off. She was a rockin' guest speaker at my sales meeting, building her self-confidence and public speaking skills. It's no wonder she aced her public speaking class in college. My team learned that our program was so duplicable, even a seven-year-old could explain it. I didn't have to teach my children about vision, intention, goal-setting, determination, and perseverance—they lived it. Without really thinking about it, I was grooming them to be future Visionistas.

As my business grew, I brought in a part-time assistant. She did the "busy" things so that I could do the "building" things. That was before we had online ordering, e-mail, Facebook,

Twitter, and iPhones. Now I can run my business from anywhere. Since my training workshops were in my home, my family attended all of them. Lauren and Alyssa helped me get ready by setting up the food and beverage "station," as well as lighting all the candles. I had a lot of candles. My daughters tell me that they have fond memories of walking in the door from school, greeted by the sweet smell of the raspberry candles I had burned all day, along with my favorite music playing (usually Hootie and the Blowfish or The Cranberries) in the background. Candles and music gave me (and my family) balance.

Mornings have never been "my thing" so I was not the kind of mom who woke up early and made pancakes for breakfast. Lauren got very good at making the morning coffee for Bill when she was in high school. As soon as she could reach the washer, she was doing her own laundry. Good thing Lauren was in the top percentile for height. There was always an expectation that running our household, and our family business, was a team effort. Responsibility is a petri dish for confidence and self-esteem. My children learned many skills, including how to set a table, light a candle, use a flip chart, set up for a meeting, create an agenda, give recognition, and give a motivational speech. Go team!

Lauren joined DECA in high school, the International Association of Marketing Students, even though her only sales and marketing experience was as a pizza server. Turns out she was a great Leader and excelled at the regional and state marketing competitions. By her senior year, she was on the Executive Board. She graduated college with a double major, Psychology/Sociology, and announced during her senior break that instead of going into the Psy D program, her new "intention" was to be a Pharmaceutical Sales Rep. Lauren never said, I'm going to "try" to do it. She just assumed she could do it. The mom in me was thinking, "How are you going to accomplish that without a science degree or sales experience?" But I kept my inner mom quiet. At the fourth interview, they asked her to come back the next day and "sell" the VP on a product of her choice. She went back to her apartment, rounded up her tealight candles, and was back the next day with free samples for all. Sampling really does work! Lauren sold the VP and became the first sales rep they ever hired fresh out of college with no prior sales experience. Today, at the age of twenty-six, she's one of the top ten reps in the nation. The VP made a great decision.

Alyssa, the youngest, was always my "little helper." During high school, she came to all my Regional Meetings and helped me unpack, set up the room, and ran all the music. When I started planning Regional Conferences with 300 to 500 attendees, she graduated from "DJ" to producer, creating the PowerPoint presentations, timing the music, and meeting with the guest speakers to review their speeches and bullet points. Her dream was to work in New York City. She turned her laptop into a vision board by using a NYC skyline picture as her screensaver. Alyssa told me she had to go to college near NYC, to keep her dream in sight. The North Jersey College was a "suitcase school," and after two years she transferred to a local university. She took a detour on her journey but got back on the road after graduation, and by the fall was working on Fifth Avenue, across the street from Cartier. I call her "That Girl," although she's too young to know who Marlo Thomas is.

Here are a few "imperfect" tips on balancing your life's work:

Get a Crock-Pot. It's your best chance for putting food on the table. All you have to do is throw in a pound of meat with a cup of liquid (broth, beer, water), add in some frozen vegetables, and you'll look like a hero. Crock-Pots saved my marriage. As long as your family is fed, they will let you go do what you have to do.

Take time for you. You know the old saying, "When Mama ain't happy, ain't nobody happy." I like to be happy. Unlike working for someone else, when you're an Entrepreneur you get to decide your own schedule. People are always telling me to slow down and take time for myself, not knowing that I'm very good at that. My best friend, Robin, and her sister, Kim, have a name for women who take time for themselves (they are both one of them), Aunt MeMe's. I'm an Aunt MeMe, too. We embrace our Aunt MeMe-ness so much that we created The Adventures of Aunt MeMe Facebook page. My boss (me) is very good at giving me "me time," when I get to just BE. I get monthly massages, walk three miles every day, and take more getaway vacations with my girlfriends than my husband would like me to. When Alyssa turned sixteen, we took a mother-daughter trip to Paris. Oui! Oui! Bill had already planned a golf trip, and Lauren was starting college so what's a girl to do? I acted on inspiration and booked a flight to Paris. My "me time" also includes doing things that are important to me, like giving back to the community. I'm the local Director of the Blue Thong Society (Google it), a women's social networking group modeled after the Clinton Initiative. Even community service can be fun.

Set office hours. Now that I'm an empty nester, I can play Million $ Party Girl whenever I want, but when my children were growing up I needed to create boundaries for my business. When office hours were over, they had my undivided attention. I also found that by focusing my time during a specific period I got more done, rather than trying to work here, there, and everywhere in between loads of laundry. If inspired action called, I'd write it down on my to-do list and tackle it when my office was open for business. My schedule worked well, allowing time for me to do all the mommy things with my daughters like dance, basketball, room mom, and cheerleading.

Ask for help. When big projects come calling, rally the troops—you can't do it alone. My sister-in-law ran a gift basket business for a few years. During the holiday season, all ten of her nieces would pitch in to get the baskets out the door. During my busy times, I'd ask my mother and mother-in-law to help out, or I'd hire a mother's helper. Let your family know what's going on so that they can be on "red alert" and pitch in where needed. My husband knew he had to pick up the kids at activities, unstack the dishwasher, and make his own dinner on my Regional Meeting days. I was so appreciative for his support that he still unstacks the dishwasher for me, even though we're a small household of two now. It's the little things that make a woman happy. As your business grows, hire a lawyer, accountant, insurance rep, financial advisor, web designer, PR/marketing consultant, and social media expert. Network and connect with all the right people that can guide your vision to reality.

Our family has lived an amazing life, with many dreams come true. We've stood on the edge of the Grand Canyon, rode an airboat through the Everglades, hiked through a rain forest, and drove through a volcano. Bill and I continue to travel, experiencing Spain, Italy, France, Switzerland, England, Canada, Hawaii, and most of the Caribbean Islands. During the middle school years, we made family memories boating on our twenty-seven-foot Donzi Cruiser. When the kids got older, we bought a beach house and rang in the millennium by running into the ocean for the "Polar Bear Swim."

If it's true that strong social support and girlfriend circles are the key to a long happy life, then I'm going to live to be 110. Many of my Hostesses and Customers, including Debbie, April, Megan, Cait, Jackie, Kelley, Stephanie, Patty, Kristen, Nicole, and so many more, are phenomenal women who have given my life *glow*. My journey has connected me to women Entrepreneurs who inspire me every day. They are the unsung heroes, taking risks, and leading the way for the next generation. It's your turn to leap and share your gifts. We'll be there waiting to catch you if you fall. As Audrey Hepburn said, "Nothing is impossible. The word itself says, I'm possible!"

NOTES:

WHO CAN HELP

MAKE YOUR VISION A REALITY?

Resource Guide

WOMEN'S NETWORKING GROUPS

eWomen Network, National Organization
"The key to networking is learning how to converse with another person...it is the art of conversation. Picking up subtle hints about a person's interest and then asking them to share about it with you. It's about find commonalities, whether personal or business, that you can use as a bridge to connect with them in a meaningful manner. It's about asking 'How can I help you?'...not, 'What can you do for me?'"

Marilyn Kleinberg - Executive Managing Director, South Jersey
ewomennetwork.com
@eWomenNetwork

Interconnections for Women, Southern NJ
"Networking should not be on the list of bad words (or things you don't want or have to do; like go to the dentist or the gynecologist). Think of it in terms of CONNECTING. We are connecting to individuals, building and forming lasting relationships that will help foster a solid foundation for referrals. As women, we do business with other women that we know, like, and trust. So get out there and start making new connections or rebuilding old ones. Your business will thank you for it!"

Stacy McGuigan - Co-Founder
interconnectionsforwomen.org
@4Connections

Professional Women's Business Network, PA, NJ, DE, NY, MD, & DC.
"As founder of the Professional Women's Business Network, I have had the pleasure of meeting some amazing women through this group who have taken an active interest to share their expertise. Going into our fourth year, the Professional Women's Business Network has grown substantially with over 2,000 affiliate women professionals gathering from several U.S. States. The PWBN's objective is to bring women together, one meeting at a time. Join us today. We hope to see you at an upcoming event."

Phyllis Smith - Founder/Organizer
pwbn.org
@PWBN

Girl's Lunch Out, Networking Events and Twitter Parties
"At Girl's Lunch Out, we believe that networking with other women in social media and business can build strong relationships both on and off line. And, since we are all busy balancing work and home, why not find time to network over lunch? Supporting one another in a fun, network-based environment can lead to friendships, business opportunities, or new, creative ventures. We love seeing connections made at our luncheons, and hope we can continue to provide an environment that fosters creativity and the entrepreneurial spirit."

Erica Voll - Co-founder Girl's Lunch Out
www.girlslunchout.com
@girlslunchout

NAWBO, National Organization
"NAWBO membership offers women-owned businesses a national and local platform to tap into the power of an already established community of women entrepreneurs. At the national level, NAWBO touts a membership of more than 7,000 members and 70 chapters across the country; and at the local level, members are encouraged to engage actively with their local chapter to gain

access to other women business owners, leadership development opportunities and community involvement."

Contact: Tracy L Shields - President, NAWBO South Jersey Chapter
nawbo.org
@NAWBONational

Blue Thong Society, National Social Networking/Community Service
BTS Chapters meet regularly in cities across the U.S. to plan outrageous outings, festive get-togethers and fabulous efforts on behalf of the charitable causes they support. Blue Thong Society members span all age groups and come from all walks of life, yet they all share the same need to be a part of a sassy group of women with youthful spirits to connect both socially and philanthropically.

Lynn Bardowski - Local Director, South Jersey
bluethongsociety.com

Websites

Facebook.com/pages	Create a FB page
Facebook.com/marketing	FB Marketing Tips
Zite.com	Personalize Magazines
Mailchimp.com	Email Marketing
twitter.com	General
digg.com	General
Pinterest.com	General
linkedin.com	Business/Entrepreneurs
Google+	General
Meetup.com	Business/Social Networking events
Netmixer.com	Networking/Business events
cafemom.com	Moms connecting with Moms
sphinn.com	Internet Marketing
seomoz.org	SEO & Social Monitoring
youtube.com	Video channel
wikihow.com	How-to
smallbusinessbrief.com	Small Business News/How-to
technorati.com	Blogging
socialbuzzclub.com	Bloggers/Social Media
blogster.com	Blogging
authorsden.com	Bloggers/Authors
problogger.net	Blogging
copyblogger.com	Tips and Training for Content
Marketers	
cafepress.com	Create an Online store

helpareporterout.com	Free PR
startupnation.com	Entrepreneurs
fiverr.com	Hire people to do things for $5
eventbrite.com	Event marketing

41072852R00061

Made in the USA
Lexington, KY
28 April 2015